CONTEMPORARY'S

ATTRACTIONS

BOOK FOUR

BIRTHPLACES OF IDEAS

ETHEL TIERSKY
MAXINE CHERNOFF

D1517851

CB

CONTEMPORARY
BOOKS

CHICAGO

Library of Congress Cataloging-in-Publication Data

Tiersky, Ethel, 1937–
    Birthplaces of ideas / Ethel Tiersky, Maxine Chernoff.
      p.   cm. — (Contemporary's Attractions ; bk. 4)
    ISBN 0-8092-3685-0
    1. Readers—Biography.   2. English language—Textbooks for foreign
speakers.   3. United States—Biography—Problems, exercises, etc.
4. Readers—United States.   I. Chernoff, Maxine, 1952-   .
II. Title.   III. Series: Tiersky, Ethel, 1937-   Attractions ; bk. 4.
PE1127.B53T54   1994
428.6′4—dc20

94-6129
CIP

Acknowledgments

We wish to thank the following for sending us background information, answering innumerable questions by phone, and, in some cases, supplying photographs for this text.

"Earth Mother": Dr. Diana Post, Rachel Carson Council, Inc., Chevy Chase, Maryland.

"Dr. King's Dream": Curatorial Department, Center for Nonviolent Change, Atlanta, Georgia; National Civil Rights Museum, Memphis, Tennessee.

"The House That Wright Built": Tony Puttnam, architect, Taliesin Architects, Madison, Wisconsin; Suzette Lucas, Director, Special Projects, Taliesin West, Scottsdale, Arizona.

"Wizard at Work": Douglas G. Tarr, Archives Technician, National Park Service, Edison National Historic Site, West Orange, New Jersey.

"The Wright Flight": Darrell Collins, historian, National Park Service, Wright Brothers National Memorial, Manteo, North Carolina; Donna Whitman, Eastern National, Kill Devil Hills, North Carolina; Tom Durant, National Park Service, Charlestown, West Virginia.

"A Different Drummer": Dick O' Connor, The Thoreau Society, Throeau Lyceum, Concord, Massachusetts; The Walden Woods Project, Boston, Massachusetts; Marcia Moss, Curator, Concord Free Public Library, Concord, Massachusetts.

Photo Credits

Cover photos: Sketch of Edison's lightbulb, Mercury Archive/The Image Bank; Edison lightbulb, Image Bank/Michael Melford; the *Flyer*, Stock Montage, Inc.; Frank Lloyd Wright's Fallingwater, Image Bank/Michael Melford; Rachel Carson History Project, Bob Hines: 2, Shirley Briggs: 5; Bettmann Archive: 8, 16, 23, 26, 32, 37, 40, 46, 52, 54, 60, 64, 67, 79; Concord Free Public Library: 74, 83.

Published by Contemporary Books, Inc.
Two Prudential Plaza, Chicago, Illinois 60601-6790
Manufactured in the United States of America
International Standard Book Number: 0-8092-3685-0

10   9   8   7   6   5   4   3   2   1

Published simultaneously in Canada by
Fitzhenry & Whiteside
195 Allstate Parkway
Markham, Ontario L3R 4T8
Canada

CONTENTS

TO THE READER

A woman whose study of nature led to a new field in science? An inventor who patented over 500 new products? An architect who designed a house over a waterfall? A writer whose works influenced nonviolent protests in India and in America? These are just a few of the amazing people whose ideas you will learn about in *Birthplaces of Ideas*, the fourth book in the four-book reading series **Attractions**.

Attractions takes you to some of our nation's most visited sites. Each book contains six stories about famous places, things, and people—and the interesting facts behind them. Along the way, you will be able to check your understanding of what you have read. Each story closes with little-known tidbits about the city and state where the attraction is located.

- *Book One, It's Colossal*, features America's giant points of interest: the Statue of Liberty, Sears Tower, the Gateway Arch, Mount Rushmore, the Grand Canyon, and Walt Disney World.

- *Book Two, Back to the Past*, features sites that have important connections to our nation's past: Plimoth Plantation, the White House, New Orleans, the San Francisco Bay Area, the Vietnam Veterans Memorial, and the commonwealth of Puerto Rico.

- *Book Three, Sun and Games*, features the attractions of six of the country's most popular vacation spots: Las Vegas, Graceland, New Mexico, Hawaii, Hollywood, and Minnesota.

- *Book Four, Birthplaces of Ideas*, features places where some of our nation's most important social ideas and inventions began: philosopher Henry David Thoreau's Walden Pond, aviators Orville and Wilbur Wright's

Kitty Hawk, inventor Thomas Edison's New Jersey, civil rights leader Martin Luther King Jr.'s Center for Nonviolent Social Change, architect Frank Lloyd Wright's Taliesin, and conservationist Rachel Carson's Greater Washington, D.C.

The stories in **Attractions** will inform you, entertain you, surprise you, and perhaps even shock you. At the same time, you will be building your knowledge about the geography of the United States.

The map below shows the locations of the sites featured in each of the four books. Those contained in *Birthplaces of Ideas* are highlighted in blue.

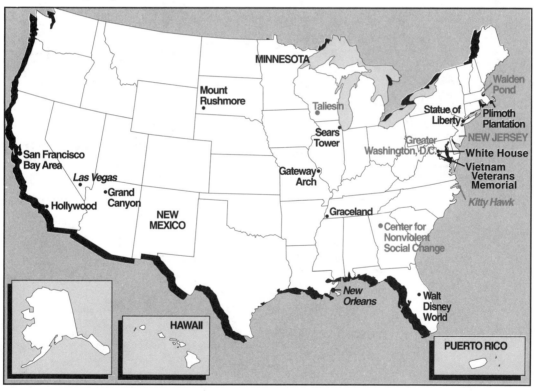

Once you've read the stories in *Birthplaces of Ideas*, we invite you to explore the other three books in the **Attractions** series. As you do, you'll learn the stories behind some of the most famous places in America.

Rachel Carson standing on her porch in Maine

EARTH MOTHER

*How did one woman's study of nature lead to a new field
in science? To find out, read on. . . .*

A Natural Writer

1   Born in Springdale, Pennsylvania, in 1907, Rachel Carson
learned to love nature at an early age. Her mother, Maria,
was a former teacher. Carson's mother took her outside and
pointed out leaves, birds, and the blue sky. "I can remember
no time when I wasn't interested in the out-of-doors and
the whole world of nature," Carson explained later.

2   Since her brother and sister were much older, Carson
was often alone as a child. She wandered around the
woods and felt less isolated. She explored the streams near
her farm. She found snake skins and robins' nests. Once
she raised a family of baby robins that had lost its mother.
Sometimes she argued with her older brother, Robert. He
liked to hunt. She asked him why he had to needlessly kill
animals. She was very convincing. He finally gave up his
hobby.

3   When Carson's brother became a soldier in World War
I, she turned her attention to the larger world. She read
about the war and talked to her parents about it. Her
brother sent her a letter. He told her about a Canadian pilot
who flew his plane even after it had lost a wing. She wrote

a story about this pilot and sent it to her favorite children's magazine, *St. Nicholas*. A year later, she received a check for $10 for her story "A Battle in the Clouds."

4   Carson was always smart in school. But she was shy and didn't have many friends. As a young girl, she published many other stories. But it was harder for her to do everyday things. For example, it took her two years of practice to get on the field hockey team. But she never gave up. She applied herself to whatever was hard for her to do. She didn't stop until she got it right.

5   After high school, Carson got a scholarship to Pennsylvania College for Women, in Pittsburgh. Carson spent her time writing and taking English classes with a favorite teacher, Miss Croff. She decided that she would become a writer. But then Carson got involved in the outdoor science classes taught by Miss Skinker. She visited state parks and beautiful forests. Her most memorable trip was to the seashore. She decided that biology, rather than writing, would be her career.

6   Many people considered her decision foolish. Few women had careers in science in the 1920s. Women were discouraged from trying to make their way in a "man's world." But because of her excellent grades, Carson received two honors: Johns Hopkins University in Maryland gave her a scholarship for graduate studies. An ocean research center in Massachusetts invited her to spend the summer studying her favorite subject, the sea.

Checking Comprehension

What shows Carson's love of nature at an early age?
How did she learn that she had a talent for writing?
Why was it more difficult for a woman to be a scientist
    than to be a writer in Carson's time?

Hardship and Triumph

7   In the late 1920s, Carson found things changing. Her father died suddenly. Her married sister died. Her sister left two small children for Carson and her mother to raise. It was also the time of the Great Depression, when economic conditions were very bad. How could a young woman scientist support a family of four?

8   Through a friend, Carson found a job at the United States Bureau of Fisheries. She wrote scripts for a radio series called "Romance Under the Water." She earned $19.25 a week. A few years later, Carson took a government exam. She was the only woman in the group, and she got the highest grade! This exam qualified her for the job of junior aquatic[1] biologist. Her income doubled. At her new job she earned $38 a week.

Carson exploring a tide pool in Maine

[1]relating to water

9   To make more money, Carson started writing in her spare time. Newspapers and magazines began publishing her articles about the sea. Some publishers in New York read her articles. They invited her to write a book based on her article "Undersea." By writing two pages a night after work, she finally finished the book *Under the Sea Wind*.

10   Soon after her book was published, bigger events took place. Her book was published a month before Japan bombed Pearl Harbor. The United States entered World War II. People turned their thoughts to the war effort. Carson's book sold fewer than 1,500 copies.

11   Her life at work changed, too. Her agency became part of the Fish and Wildlife Service. During the war, she collected a lot of information about the effects of chemicals on soldiers. She studied DDT and other chemicals invented around that time. She also edited a series of booklets that publicized a new program. Under this program, land was being set aside for plants and animals in wildlife refuges.[2] Living things were being saved from industrial expansion.

12   In preparing these booklets, Carson traveled to many of the refuges. She explored coastal Virginia and Maryland with a friend from the bureau. On this coastal trip, she began to think of a new project. Using 1,000 different sources for research, she began writing a book. It would explain the ocean and its natural wonders to the average person. To learn more about the sea, she stayed on an ocean research ship called *Albatross*[3] *II*. She was the first woman to stay on such a ship. Here she could examine unusual fish under microscopes. She could hear underwater ocean sounds through a special instrument.

---

[2]places where plants and animals are protected
[3]a large water bird similar to a seagull

13   Oxford University Press published *The Sea Around Us* in 1951. Carson became an instant celebrity. The book was so popular that it was first on the *New York Times* best-seller list for 39 weeks! Never before had a book about science done so well in the United States. Carson found her mailbox stuffed with invitations for lectures. Now she could realize her dream of being a full-time nature writer. Living in a cottage in Maine, she completed her third book, *The Edge of the Sea*, in 1955.

Checking Comprehension

Why did Carson have to find work quickly during the Great Depression?

How well did her first book sell? Why?

How well did her second book sell?

A Quiet Fighter

14   In 1957, when Carson was fifty, her grandnephew, Roger Christie, was orphaned. Carson adopted him. Taking care of a five-year-old took time away from her writing. But she already knew Roger well. She was delighted to be close to him. She kept Roger busy by taking him for walks in the woods near her Maryland home and reading stories to him. With Roger in mind, she had already written an article called "Help Your Child to Wonder." It explains in poetic language how parents can teach their children to love and respect nature. After Carson's death, this article became an illustrated book, *The Sense of Wonder*.

15   Around this time, Carson got a letter from her dear friend Olga Owens Huckins. Huckins had a large, beautiful garden. It was a sanctuary[4] for birds, in Massachusetts. But

---

[4]a place of safety

something was wrong. In order to control mosquitoes, the state had sprayed chemicals on Huckins's sanctuary. Three birds were found dead near the birdbath the next day. The following afternoon, Huckins saw a robin drop off its branch.

16   Huckins hoped that her friend could help her. For years Carson had researched the effects of pesticides[5] and written articles about them. Would Carson tell the world what was happening to her friend's beautiful songbirds?

*Carson at work
in her laboratory*

17   At that time, DDT, a powerful pesticide, was used widely by farmers and gardeners. It had been invented to fight insect pests. In fact, its inventor had won the Nobel Prize in 1948. Though DDT was effective in controlling insects, it also had many bad effects. When birds ate insects exposed to DDT, the pesticide got into the birds' systems. When other animals ate the birds, they also ate the DDT. Plants got sprayed as well. If animals or people ate these plants, they also ate DDT.

---

[5]chemicals used to kill insects

18   People did not understand how everything in our environment is related. They did not realize that all plants, animals, and people live in an ecosystem.[6] They did not see how killing an insect with a chemical or using a weed killer could affect human beings. Ideas we accept today were not recognized then. The word *ecology* had not even been invented yet!

19   How could Carson help her friend and her planet? First, she wrote an article about pesticides and sent it to some popular magazines. No magazine would take it. They questioned her ideas. They doubted that a female scientist could be right. They worried that their advertisers, who made some of these chemicals, might be upset.

20   Carson did more research. She collected information and followed an important court case. Oily DDT spray was killing fish, crabs, and birds on Long Island, in New York. "There will be no peace for me if I keep silent," she said. Carson also worked on other projects. She finished her fourth book, *Silent Spring*, in 1962. An important magazine, *The New Yorker*, published parts of it. *Silent Spring* became a bestseller. Millions of people read about how dangerous pesticides were poisoning the earth and killing the beautiful spring songbirds.

Checking Comprehension

Why did Olga Owens Huckins write to her friend Carson?

Why was Carson a good person for Huckins to contact?

What facts about the environment were unknown at the time?

---

[6]a system in which all living elements and their environment are related

21   Not everyone was pleased with Carson's book. Chemical companies threatened to sue the publisher. The U.S. government spent $250,000 to defend the use of pesticides in farming. People who opposed Carson called her names, including "bird lover," "hysterical woman," and "communist." Cartoons were published in newspapers showing insects taking over the earth.

22   Carson received hundreds of letters about the book. She had to write ten different form letters to answer her mail. Her secretary sent out the most fitting letter to each person. But one letter Carson received was especially important. It came from the U.S. Congress. President John F. Kennedy had set up a committee to study pesticide use. Carson was invited to talk to the committee. She spoke quietly and forcefully. She knew her facts and presented them well.

23   People who defended Carson included important writers and scientists. Supreme Court Justice William O. Douglas loved nature. He called *Silent Spring* the most important book of the century. He said she was a genius. Suddenly, to some, she was a prophet.[7] She cautioned that everything on earth was related. Toxic chemicals, she warned, while killing insect pests, might also destroy humankind. Her message was threefold: Progress is not always positive. People need to be aware of the possible dangers. People have to question new solutions to old problems.

24   Carson's views were unpopular in an era when synthetics[8] like plastic, vinyl, and DDT had recently been invented.

---

[7]someone who predicts the future
[8]products made with chemicals

But time has shown that Carson's views were right. She was a rare person, a scientist whose concern extended to all humankind. Her laboratory was the world. As more people studied her research, they came to agree that better solutions had to be found. In explaining how DDT worked its way into the environment, she guided a whole generation.

25   Today, everyone understands the connections of plant, animal, and human life on earth. Scientists who read her works invented the study of ecology. Today, many people see Carson as a bold pioneer. All are grateful for her vision.

Checking Comprehension

Why were people reluctant to believe that progress could be harmful?

What new field did Carson play a key role in founding?

Tributes and Landmarks

26   More and more people became interested in the dangers of pesticides. Organizations began giving Rachel Carson important awards for her work. The one that made her most proud was the Albert Schweitzer [Shwhite'sir] Medal of the Animal Welfare Institute. Many more nature groups gave her honors.

27   Some television specials dealt with the subject of *Silent Spring*. "CBS Reports" did a special show on pesticides. Americans learned that 900 million pounds of pesticides had been spread around the United States in 1963 alone.

28   As Carson became more famous, she felt very proud that her concerns were being heard. As she struggled with illness, it helped her to know that her important work would be remembered. Though she was only in her fifties, she knew she was dying, of cancer. She also knew that she had succeeded in her life's work.

29   Soon after her death, in 1964, friends set up a living tribute to Carson's memory. The Rachel Carson Council was founded in 1965 in Chevy Chase, Maryland. The council studies the effects of chemicals on the planet. It encourages people to use safe methods to control insect pests. In 1970, a new government agency was established to protect the environment. The Environmental Protection Agency (EPA) monitors[9] our country's air, land, and water. It owes its existence to Carson's ideas.

30   Three sites have been dedicated to Carson's memory. Her childhood home in Pennsylvania is a historic landmark. On the coast of Maine, where she spent some of her summers, is a Rachel Carson Wildlife Refuge.

31   Carson's home was in Silver Spring, Maryland, a suburb of Washington, D.C. In 1993, it became a National Historic Landmark. Carson lived there while she researched *Silent Spring*. She designed and supervised construction of the red brick house on an acre of land. She lived there for 26 years. Inside the house, there is a special mirrored shelf she used for her seashell collection. She also took special care to landscape the grounds with large wooded areas and a natural garden. In spring, daffodils and pink and white azaleas [uh·zay'lee·uhs] decorate the front. People can drive up and see the place where this great woman lived and worked.

Checking Comprehension

What did the television report reveal about DDT use in the United States?

What three sites are dedicated to Rachel Carson?

---

[9]records the condition of and provides controls for

SIDELIGHTS

About Rachel Carson

- Listed among the 100 most important Americans in the 20th century
- Member of the Environmental Hall of Fame
- Received the National Book Award for *The Sea Around Us*
- First woman to receive the John Burroughs Geography Medal, in 1951
- Awarded our nation's highest honor, the Presidential Medal of Freedom, in 1980
- Featured on a U.S. postage stamp in 1981

About Maryland, the Old Line State

- Maryland was first called the Old Line State and the Free State by General George Washington, for the bravery of its soldiers during the American Revolution.
- It was a border state between the North and the South during the Civil War. Today, the northern part is industrial. The southern part has fine old mansions, tobacco farms, and a slower pace of life.
- Its population is 4.7 million.
- Popular tourist attractions include horse racing at Pimlico, Fort McHenry, Antietam Battlefield (site of early Civil War battles), Edgar Allan Poe House, Babe Ruth's birthplace, and the home of Rachel Carson (in Montgomery County).

Making Inferences

Reread the paragraph(s) indicated after each statement. Then decide if each statement is probably true or false.

_____ 1. Carson was lonely as a child because she loved nature. (paragraphs 1–2)

_____ 2. Carson's first book did not sell well because it wasn't very good. (paragraphs 9–10)

_____ 3. Carson did careful research to write *The Sea Around Us*. (paragraphs 12–13)

_____ 4. When the inventor of DDT won the Nobel Prize, scientists knew everything about the chemical he had invented. (paragraphs 17–18)

_____ 5. Carson made new connections between chemicals and their effects. (paragraph 20)

_____ 6. People disagreed about the value of *Silent Spring*. (paragraphs 21–23)

_____ 7. Scientists who followed Carson all studied pesticides. (paragraphs 24–25)

Practicing Vocabulary

Circle the correct word(s) to complete each sentence.

1. People who study aquatic life work near (an ocean, a forest, a mountain, a desert).
2. Those interested in ecology want to know how plants and animals are (studied, related, separated, killed).
3. On a coastal trip, travelers look out of a car window and see (valleys, mountains, the desert, the shore).
4. In studying pesticides, Carson learned that some of their effects were (creative, deadly, interesting, popular).
5. It was not easy for women to study (art, writing, the science of life, garden styles) in the 1920s.

6. When Carson's dream was realized, it (came true, was finished, was understood, was sold).
7. Synthetic products are (natural, real, man-made, beneficial).

Talking It Over

1. Scientists don't always know where their discoveries may lead. What would you do if you were a scientist who had invented something that might hurt people or nature?
2. Do you believe it's necessary for technology to advance even when it may do harm?
3. How do you show your appreciation for nature? How do you teach children to appreciate it?
4. What advice would you give to a young woman who wants to do something unusual? Are some careers more appropriate for women than others?
5. Think of an area in your community that has an ecological problem. What are some solutions to the problem?

Dr. Martin Luther King Jr. in a pensive mood

DR. KING'S DREAM

The nation's best-known human rights leader was identified by the wrong name on his birth certificate. How could this have happened? To find out, read on. . . .

Sweet Auburn

1 The son of a minister and a former teacher who played piano and organ, Martin Luther King Jr. was born in Atlanta, Georgia, on January 15, 1929. To distinguish him from his father, little Martin was called M.L. The King family lived in a stately, handsome, two-story house on Auburn Avenue. The area was called Sweet Auburn by residents. It was a comfortable place to grow up—a well-to-do African-American neighborhood. This neighborhood had the first black-owned radio station in the country. It also had the oldest black-run life insurance company. African-American doctors, ministers, and teachers mixed freely on the street with workers and store clerks.

2 But blacks and whites did not live together in Atlanta. Laws stated that the races could not mix in hotels, in restaurants, on public transportation, and in schools. These laws, called Jim Crow laws, created segregation. Signs told what public facilities blacks and whites could use. For African-Americans who thought these laws were unfair and

did not follow them, there was constant danger, even death.

3   When King was a child, he began to notice these divisions. Once, when he was about six, a white woman told him that he could no longer play with her sons because he was black. King felt sad, but his parents were very wise. At home, they stressed the importance of discipline and of love. They provided him with lots of good examples. Even before he was old enough for school, he read books. He read about Africa, slavery, the Civil War, and black heroes like Harriet Tubman and Frederick Douglass. As a child, King staged one of his first protests. It was against doing the dishes. He thought it was "woman's work"!

4   Very early, King realized two important things: To succeed in life, he would have to study very hard. He would also have to be a good Christian. From his teacher mother, he learned the importance of devotion to daily tasks. From his minister father, he learned about the power of words to inspire people. In high school, King joined the debate team. He practiced using words to win arguments. He also watched his father as he worked in the community on behalf of his members at the Ebenezer Baptist Church.

5   Today, one block west of King's childhood home is the Center for Nonviolent Social Change. For King's widow, Coretta Scott King, it is home away from home. Since her husband's death, it has been her goal to see his dreams of peaceful change fulfilled. Scholars from around the country study at the center. The center sponsors programs to promote change through nonviolence at many colleges and universities.

6   Visitors can learn at the center as well. They can see handwritten copies of King's letters and speeches. They can look at the suitcase and travel alarm that he carried on so many journeys. They can see his tie tack and cuff links and wallet. When they spot the key to room 307 of the Lorraine Hotel they pause for a moment. They think of his shooting.

They think of that terrible night in Memphis in April 1968 when so many Americans felt sadness and despair because King had been killed.

7 Visitors then step out into the courtyard of the large complex. They see the place where the great man is buried. They read the inscription on the crypt:[1] "Free at last. Free at last. Thank God Almighty I'm free at last."

Checking Comprehension

What was King's first experience with racial prejudice?

What did King learn from his parents?

What was Coretta Scott King's goal after her husband's death?

The Early Years

8 When he was only 15, King began college in Atlanta. He attended Morehouse College, where his father had gone. He thought about becoming a lawyer or a doctor. He gave his first sermon at his father's church when he was 17. King did very well, and his father was extremely proud. At 18, he became a minister, and at 19, he graduated college.

9 Then he went north to Philadelphia to study more about the ministry. He kept the bitter lessons of Jim Crow in his mind even in the North, where African-Americans and whites mixed more freely.

10 King read and studied about the great Indian leader Mohandas Gandhi [Moe·hahn′dis Gahn′dee]. Gandhi was using nonviolent methods to win India's freedom from the British. Gandhi thought that it was an honor to be jailed for a just cause. He preached against using weapons or physical force to win changes in society.

---

[1] a vault in which a person is buried underground

11   King also read the writings of New Englander Henry David Thoreau [Thor·oh']. Thoreau's essay "Civil Disobedience" explained how to peacefully object to unjust laws and customs. These beliefs would be important to King in leading the civil rights movement in the South.

12   While taking more courses at Boston University and Harvard, King met a young African-American woman. Her name was Coretta Scott. Like King, she had experienced racial injustice in the South in a very personal way. Her house was burned down in a fire caused by a white arsonist. Also, her father's sawmill was burnt down when he refused to sell it. Martin and Coretta married in 1953. King became the pastor of the Dexter Avenue Baptist Church in Montgomery, Alabama. Coretta Scott King understood what life in the South would be like. She became King's partner in his struggles.

Checking Comprehension

What did King notice about life in the North?
What did Gandhi and Thoreau teach King?
Why was Coretta Scott a good partner for King?

---

13   Years of education and a passionate belief in equality led King to become involved in many causes. When African-American Rosa Parks refused to give up her seat on a bus to a white passenger, she was arrested. King helped to organize a protest. African-Americans who rode the bus would boycott[2] public transportation in the city.

14   For 382 days, nearly 100 percent of Montgomery's African-Americans—50,000 in all—walked to work or formed car pools. Because the boycott was so successful, someone threw a bomb at King's house. An angry crowd gathered, but King calmed them down. He called on his Christian faith and Gandhi's teachings about nonviolence. He stated that hatred must be fought with love. Rosa Parks's brave action and King's ability to lead the movement made this case very important. Finally, it went to the Supreme Court. Dedication led to justice. In 1956, the highest court said that segregated buses were unconstitutional.[3] Southern buses had to be integrated.

15   King continued working tirelessly for civil rights. In one year alone, 1957, he traveled about 780,000 miles. He made 208 speeches in favor of freedom and equal rights for African-Americans. He and other ministers formed the Southern Christian Leadership Conference (SCLC) to fight unfair laws in the South. He led sit-ins[4] at segregated lunch counters, theaters, libraries, and schools.

16   Back in Atlanta, in 1960, King became the assistant pastor of his father's church. Working with the SCLC, he organized freedom rides through the South beginning in 1961. Both black and white civil rights workers rode buses

---

[2]to refuse to use, buy, or deal with as a means of protest
[3]not allowed by the law of the land
[4]nonviolent protests where people block the use of facilities

through the South. They sat together in "whites only" waiting rooms. They drank together at "whites only" water fountains. Often they were attacked by angry crowds and refused help by the police. The worst attack occurred in Montgomery, Alabama. Police dogs and high-powered hoses were turned on the demonstrators.

17 Finally, the federal government called in troops to protect the freedom riders. King needed protection, too. One time, he was preaching in a Montgomery church. A white mob waited outside. "We shall overcome someday," people sang all night in the church as King led them in prayer.

18 Today, a beautiful monument, the Civil Rights Memorial, stands in Montgomery, Alabama. Built in 1989, this fountain of black granite is engraved with famous biblical words. King spoke them about freedom: "We will not be satisfied until justice rolls down like waters and righteousness like a mighty stream." Water flows over the names of 40 martyrs[5] to the cause of civil rights, including King's.

Checking Comprehension

What was the result of the Montgomery bus boycott?

What were some activities of the SCLC?

How is the civil rights movement marked in Montgomery today?

---

[5]people who lose their lives working for an important cause

A Prize for Peace

19   On August 28, 1963, more than 200,000 Americans gathered in the nation's capital for the March on Washington. They listened to King deliver his famous "I Have a Dream" speech. Blacks and whites stood together as King described an America where everyone would be free and equal. Millions more watched television or listened to radio as his words rang out. People were moved by the emotion in his voice as he called for peaceful change.

King leading the March on Washington

20   Attempts to integrate the South were met by many violent reactions. In Birmingham, Alabama, King was organizing marches for freedom. A church was bombed. Four African-American girls attending Sunday school were killed. Several months later, when President Kennedy was assassinated,[6] King made this prophecy[7] to his wife, "I'll never live to see 40."

---

[6]murdered by a surprise or secret attack
[7]a prediction of a future event

21   There followed a summer of more nonviolent protests and more deaths of innocent people. Three white college students working for voters' rights in the South were killed. King felt very tired and sad. He checked into a hospital to rest. Meanwhile, he received an important phone call from his wife. For his work in the field of civil rights, the 35-year-old King became the youngest person ever to receive the Nobel Peace Prize.

22   King traveled to Europe to accept this award and the $54,600 it came with. He was very proud, but he did not keep the large sum of money for himself. He gave it to organizations working for racial equality in the United States. He made a speech accepting the prize. He said, "This prize belongs to all men who love peace and brotherhood."

23   Shortly after that, King was needed back in Alabama. There he led a 50-mile march of blacks and whites. They crossed the Edmund Pettus Bridge, in Selma, Alabama, on their way to Montgomery. The march was organized to gain voting rights for African-Americans. King had to walk past jeering crowds and angry Alabama state troopers. Despite his awards and fame, King had to confront danger every day.

Checking Comprehension

How many people heard King's famous speech either in person or by watching him on television?

What was King's dream for America?

What was important to him about winning the Nobel Prize?

A Prophecy Fulfilled

24   After winning the Nobel Peace Prize, King became a national leader. He was called to the White House to meet with the president. He helped President Lyndon Johnson build support for the Voting Rights Act of 1965. It guaranteed equality at the polls[8] for African-Americans.

25   In 1966, King and his family moved for a short time to an apartment in the North Lawndale neighborhood of Chicago. He began to focus on another problem for many Americans, poverty. For there to be real equality in the United States, all people needed economic opportunity. People needed to live decent lives. King's work on poverty issues continued for several years. He wanted to have another march on Washington. This march would unite poor people of all ethnic groups: African-Americans, whites, Mexican-Americans, Puerto Ricans, and Native Americans.

26   While planning this march, in April of 1968, he traveled to Memphis, Tennessee, to help African-American garbage workers. They were demanding equal pay. In Memphis, on April 4, shots rang out while King stood on the balcony of the Lorraine Hotel. King's tragic prophecy was fulfilled. He died at age 39. Later, James Earl Ray, a white supremacist[9] and escaped convict, was convicted of the murder.

27   When Dr. Martin Luther King Jr. was killed, many African-Americans felt great despair. There were riots in many major cities. Many angry and saddened people ques-

---

[8]places where people go to vote
[9]someone who believes in the superiority of the white race

tioned whether nonviolence was the best way to solve the racial divisions in the United States. But the nonviolent legacy of the civil rights movement has continued.

Checking Comprehension

How did King help President Johnson?
Why did King want to march on Washington a second time?

Memories of the Movement

28   On July 4, 1993, civil rights leaders including Coretta Scott King and the Reverend Jesse Jackson went to Memphis. They gave speeches and attended ceremonies. They visited Mason Temple, where King gave his last speech. They remembered and discussed the civil rights movement. Recalling King, they had mixed emotions. They were glad that the National Civil Rights Museum was about to be dedicated. And they were sad that the great leader could not be there to enjoy the event.

King delivering his "I Have a Dream" speech

29   For many years, people in Memphis wanted to mark the site where King lost his life, the Lorraine Hotel. Could the site of such a terrible tragedy be turned into a memorial? The state of Tennessee, the city of Memphis, Shelby County, and many private citizens donated the $9.2 million needed for the museum to be built. Most of the structure is new, but architects have preserved the facade[10] of the Lorraine Hotel.

30   Behind that facade is a wonderful museum. It celebrates King's life and the civil rights movement. Ten thousand square feet of exhibits tell the dramatic story of how marches, demonstrations, sit-ins, and speeches changed the course of American history.

31   A videotape introduces 15 exhibits from the civil rights era. They are arranged in chronological[11] order. The first exhibit explains the *Brown v. Board of Education of Topeka* ruling of 1954. This important court case desegregated the Topeka, Kansas, schools. It made separating black and white students against the law. At another exhibit, visitors can go into a Montgomery, Alabama, bus. They can sit where Rosa Parks sat on the day she refused to give up her seat to a white person.

32   Several other interesting exhibits illustrate King's importance. One exhibit is a model of the Birmingham, Alabama, jail cell where he wrote his famous letter in 1963. This eloquent[12] letter stated that unjust laws should be broken peacefully so that justice can be established. King's famous "I Have A Dream" speech plays on the soundtrack at another exhibit.

---

[10]face of a building
[11]according to time, beginning with the earliest
[12]beautifully written or spoken

33   Some people wonder about one exhibit. They're not sure whether they like it or not. It is a laser sculpture that traces the fatal bullet's path to the Lorraine Hotel balcony from a boardinghouse across the street.

34   Perhaps the most moving exhibit is another work of art. It is a traditional bronze sculpture in the museum's lobby. *Movement to Overcome* features human figures clinging to a rock and struggling upward. It shows the bravery of all people involved in the civil rights movement. It is a tribute to the dedicated and inspired work of Dr. Martin Luther King Jr.

Checking Comprehension

Why did civil rights leaders gather on July 4, 1993?

Did King think that all laws should be obeyed?

What two sculptures are in the National Civil Rights
   Museum?

SIDELIGHTS

About Dr. Martin Luther King Jr.

- On his birth certificate, he was mistakenly called Michael. When he was five, his family corrected the birth certificate.
- King's mother's father, Alfred Daniel Williams, had also been the pastor of the Ebenezer Baptist Church.
- King had two childhood nicknames, Tweed, for the suits he wore, and Will Shoot, because he shot the basketball every time he got it.

About Atlanta

- Atlanta is Georgia's state capital.
- Founded in 1837, 90 percent of Atlanta was burned by the Union army, led by General William T. Sherman.
- It has 29 universities.
- It is the home of the Jimmy Carter Library.
- It is the site of the 1996 Summer Olympics.
- The nation's largest airport, Hartsfield International, is located in Atlanta.

About Georgia, the Peach State

- Population: 6,500,000
- Fourth of the 13 original states
- A leading producer of peaches
- Largest state east of the Mississippi and largest of the southern states

Making Inferences

Reread the paragraph(s) indicated after each statement. Then decide if each statement is probably true or false.

_____ 1. Young King was always obedient at home. (paragraph 3)

_____ 2. Young King believed that knowledge and faith were keys to success. (paragraph 4)

_____ 3. Coretta Scott King was a good partner because she was also a minister. (paragraph 12)

_____ 4. King's nonviolent teachings could always prevent violence. (paragraphs 14, 17, 20–21, 26)

_____ 5. Sit-ins take place at lunch counters only. (paragraph 15)

_____ 6. King's prophecy about his life was correct. (paragraphs 20, 26)

_____ 7. Some people don't think that the laser sculpture in the National Civil Rights Museum is a good idea because it cost too much money. (paragraph 33)

Practicing Vocabulary

Circle the correct word to complete each sentence.

1. King decided to become a (minister, lawyer, doctor, trooper) after preaching at his father's church.
2. When people participate in a bus boycott, they (fight, demonstrate, refuse, agree) to ride the bus.
3. Martyrs are people who (scare, offer, sacrifice, win) their lives.
4. The Voting Rights Act (guaranteed, dedicated, refused, demonstrated) equality at the polls for all Americans.
5. On July 4, 1993, people attended ceremonies to (demonstrate, celebrate, protest, award) the completion of the new Civil Rights Museum.

6. The museum exhibits are arranged in (dramatic, visual, nonviolent, chronological) order.
7. After King's death, many Americans felt (violence, nonviolence, despair, memory).
8. Coretta Scott King has (guaranteed, dedicated, demonstrated, refused) her life to her husband's nonviolent teachings.

Talking It Over

1. Do you think it was a good idea to build the Civil Rights Museum on the site of the former Lorraine Hotel? Why or why not?
2. Do you agree with King that knowledge and religious faith lead to success? Are other ingredients important? What are they?
3. Have you ever participated in a protest or boycott? What was the issue? Do you think that people should participate in boycotts?
4. If Martin Luther King Jr. were alive today, how do you think he would judge American society?
5. Have you ever put yourself in personal danger for a belief? What was the result?
6. Do you agree with Dr. and Mrs. King that nonviolence is the best way to change society? Why or why not?

Frank Lloyd Wright at the Capitol

THE HOUSE THAT WRIGHT BUILT

Frank Lloyd Wright designed about 500 buildings. How many of them are still standing? To find out, read on. . . .

Shining Brow

1   Ancient Greek legend tells of a beautiful bird that never really died. At the end of its long life cycle, the phoenix [fee'nix] would burn itself up in a fire. Then a young, beautiful phoenix would spring from the ashes. Frank Lloyd Wright's Taliesin [Tal·ee·es'in] showed that same spirit. After each disaster,[1] this famous house was reborn with a fresh, new beauty.

2   The Taliesin complex covers a picturesque[2] 600-acre area near Spring Green, Wisconsin. In the summer, the hills are deep green. The blue pond is dotted with graceful white geese. A waterfall completes the lovely country scene. It looks like the perfect home for an artist. It doesn't seem like a setting for violence and tragedy. But this house has been both.

---

[1]something that happens suddenly and causes much suffering
[2]like a picture, scenic, showing the beauty of nature

3   For 48 years, Taliesin was the home and studio of Frank Lloyd Wright, one of America's greatest architects.[3] Before that, the land it's on was part of a family farm. Wright's maternal grandparents moved to Spring Green from Wales. They fell in love with the beautiful valley near the Wisconsin River. Wright's grandfather bought land there for a family home and farm.

4   Wright was born in Wisconsin in 1867. Even before his birth, his mother decided that her son would be an architect. To encourage this interest, she hung pictures of famous churches above his crib. She also bought him special architectural building blocks, which he often played with. Young Frank spent summers on the family farm. There, he learned to love nature and to appreciate the beauty of natural materials.

5   Young Frank often thought about building a house on his favorite hill at the farm. He felt that a house shouldn't be on top of a hill, like a hat on a person's head. Instead, it should seem a natural part of the hill, like the brow, or forehead, on a person's face. Many years later, Wright built his home on the brow of the hill. He named the house Taliesin. It means "shining brow" in Welsh. Taliesin is also the name of a Welsh poet who loved the fine arts.

Checking Comprehension

What did Wright learn from life on the farm?
Why didn't Wright like a house on top of a hill?

---

[3]persons who design buildings and advise in their construction

The Chicago Years

6   During his young adult years, school and then work took Wright away from Spring Green. For about two years, he studied engineering at the University of Wisconsin. Then, in 1887, he left school and went to Chicago. Soon, he became chief draftsman[4] for two famous men, Dankmar Adler, an engineer, and Louis Sullivan, an architect. Wright's later work showed the influence of Sullivan's ideas. Sullivan believed that form should follow function. In other words, the design of a building should reflect its use.

7   While working for Adler and Sullivan, Wright had agreed not to take on any other assignments. But, to make extra money, he began to build bootleg[5] houses. When his employers found out, they were quite angry. As a result, in 1893, Wright went into business for himself.

8   By then, Wright was married and living with his family in Oak Park, Illinois, a suburb of Chicago. During his Chicago years, he designed many homes for the flat midwestern landscape. His style, copied by others, came to be called the prairie style. His houses were low and horizontal. Wright used wood and other natural materials from the area to tie his houses to their environment.

9   Wright lived and worked in Oak Park for 20 years. The suburb still has 33 of his buildings, including his home and studio. Visitors on walking tours are a frequent sight there.

---

[4]a person who makes accurate architectural drawings
[5]something made secretly and unlawfully

Among Wright's Oak Park buildings is Unity Temple. It was innovative[6] because its concrete construction showed on the outside. When other architects had used concrete, they had covered it with other material. But Wright's buildings did not.

Checking Comprehension

What does "form should follow function" mean?

How did his family's farm influence Wright's architecture?

What was unusual about Wright's Unity Temple?

Scandal

10   In 1909, when he was 42 years old, Wright was a successful, well-known architect. Ten assistants worked with him. But he risked losing everything for love. Wright left his wife and six children and went to Europe with another woman. Her name was Mamah Cheney [May'muh Chay'nee]. They met when Cheney's husband hired Wright to design the Cheney home. Mamah Cheney left her two children with their father to go with Wright. The scandal cost Wright many clients.

11   A year later, Wright and Cheney returned from Europe. Wright's mother gave him her portion of the family farm near Spring Green. Wright began to build his home on the brow of the hill.

12   The building fit its surroundings in many ways. The lines of the roofs followed the lines of the hills. The building's stone came from a nearby quarry. Porches connected the indoors and outdoors. Inside, there were 21 fireplaces.

---

[6]something new, a change

They were centers of warmth and social activity. Taliesin was spacious and yet cozy. By 1911, the building was complete. Wright and Cheney moved into their new home.

Checking Comprehension

Why did Wright build his home near Spring Green?
How did Taliesin connect the outdoors and the indoors?
How did the Cheney scandal affect Wright's business?

Tragedy at Taliesin

13   On August 15, 1913, Wright and his son John, also an architect, were working on a project in Chicago. On this day, a tragedy was to take place at Taliesin. Two months before, Wright had hired a cook. He couldn't get along with the other workers, so Cheney had fired him. August 15th was to be his last day at Taliesin.

Taliesin in Spring Green, Wisconsin

14   Six Taliesin employees were having lunch in the dining room that day. Cheney and her two children were having lunch by the pond. After serving the soup, the fired cook poured gasoline on the dining room rugs and lit a match. Then he ran outdoors with an ax and killed everyone he could. Only the gardener and the carpenter survived. After the murders, the crazed cook killed himself.

15   In Chicago, the great architect received word of trouble and hurried home. When Wright reached Taliesin that night, he found about half of the house burned down. Many of his valuable works of art were destroyed. Seven people had been murdered, including the woman he loved.

16   When he saw what had happened, Wright's despair and loneliness overwhelmed[7] him. He found some comfort in rebuilding Taliesin. To erase painful memories, he made changes in the house. To finance this remodeling, he accepted new projects. By late 1915, Taliesin was rebuilt. But in 1925, an electrical fire did $200,000 worth of damage to Taliesin. Wright borrowed money to rebuild Taliesin once again.

17   Not long after the first Taliesin fire, a sculptor named Miriam Noel wrote to offer her sympathy. Soon after that, she and Wright met. Noel was an attractive, sophisticated,[8] and temperamental[9] woman. In 1923, Wright married her. At midnight on a chilly November evening, the bride and groom stood in the exact center of the bridge over the Wisconsin River. That act stood for the bridging of their differences. But the marriage ended in divorce.

---

[7]overpowered in thought or feeling
[8]worldly
[9]easily upset, moody

18   In 1928, Wright married Oglivanna Hinzenberg, a native of Montenegro [Mahn·ten·ee′grow],[10] with whom he had a daughter. These two remained happily married until his death in 1959, a few months before his 92nd birthday.

Checking Comprehension

What caused the first Taliesin fire? The second?

How did Taliesin help Wright recover from tragedy?

Taliesin Today

19   Taliesin was always being worked on. For this reason, the house is probably the best example of Wright's many architectural ideas. Many experts also consider it his finest building. Wright's love of nature and the Orient[11] are easily seen, even from the outside of the house. One of the building's striking features is its birdwalk, which Wright added for Hinzenberg. The birdwalk, a cantilever [can′ti·lee·ver],[12] seems to hang, unsupported, in midair. It reaches out 40 feet from the living room over the treetops. Taliesin also has many other outdoor areas where people can sit and enjoy the scenery, gardens, fountains, and Asian sculptures. One patio has a huge Oriental bell. Years ago, it was rung to announce afternoon tea.

20   As with many of Wright's homes, the entrance of Taliesin is somewhat dark and hidden. This feature creates an air of privacy and mystery. But, entering the huge house, visitors find an enormous, two-story living room. Panels of windows let in the light and show the beautiful Wisconsin scenery. Most of the floor is made of wood and stone and covered with brightly colored Oriental carpets. Wright's

---

[10]a small eastern European country
[11]countries in the Eastern hemisphere
[12]a part of a building that projects out of the main part

trademark color, sometimes called Taliesin red, highlights the room. Electric lighting is indirect, bounced off the ceiling, for a natural look. Textures and fabrics are varied and interesting. The living room is the most famous room in the house. One Wright scholar called it "a constant visual delight."

Spacious living room at Taliesin

21   Taliesin continues to be reborn. In 1990, a fund-raising campaign began to raise $20 million for repairing Taliesin and improving the site's tourist facilities. The Frank Lloyd Wright Foundation expects that, by the year 2000, Taliesin will welcome about 200,000 visitors a year.

22   Even today, large crowds tour the buildings and grounds in the summer. In addition, artists and students live and work on the property. Members of Taliesin Associated Architects teach students enrolled in the Frank Lloyd Wright School of Architecture. The program is also called the Taliesin Fellowship.

23   The Taliesin Fellowship was established by Wright and his third wife in 1932. It gives students apprenticeships[13]

---

[13]learning by doing jobs with experienced workers

rather than a traditional college experience. Applications come in from all parts of the world. There is always a waiting list because yearly enrollment in the school is limited to 35 students. Students work with an equal number of faculty members. Tuition and room and board are quite low. As part of their apprenticeship, students work on architectural projects. The school, which awards a master's degree in architecture, operates year-round. Students and faculty are at Taliesin in Spring Green during the summer and at Taliesin West, in Scottsdale, Arizona, for the rest of the year.

Checking Comprehension

Why is Taliesin still a busy place?

How does the Taliesin Fellowship differ from a typical college experience?

Why do you think the architectural school has two sites?

What Wright Built

24   During his 70-year career, Wright created about 1,100 designs for homes, schools, churches, hotels, theaters, museums, and office buildings. About 500 of his structures were actually built, and 409 are still standing. Wright also designed furniture, glassware, and fabrics.

25   One of Wright's most famous buildings was the Imperial Hotel in Tokyo, Japan. Through one major earthquake and several smaller ones, the Imperial Hotel stood its ground. It proved that this great architect was also a great engineer.

26   Wright's engineering skills were also apparent in the design of the Pennsylvania home called Fallingwater. The amazing house was built over a waterfall. After Wright drew the designs, his client sent them to another architect

for a second opinion. That architect wrote back that the building would be unsafe. A little worried, the client sent the letter to Wright. Wright's response? Anyone who believed such nonsense didn't deserve to own a Frank Lloyd Wright home. Fallingwater, built in 1936, hasn't slipped into the waterfall yet.

27   Wright's Guggenheim Museum in New York City (completed after his death) has been praised and cursed. Most admire its unique beauty. Lit up at night, this round building looks like a spaceship about to take off. Inside, visitors walk down a continuous[14] spiral ramp from the top floor to street level. Because the floor isn't level, some say it's not a good space for viewing art. But it reflects Wright's idea of making a structure a continuous whole.

28   Of all his buildings, which did Wright consider his greatest accomplishment? "The next one, of course," Wright once told a television interviewer.

29   Wright's influence led to great changes in American architecture. He used glass, concrete, cantilevers, and indirect lighting in new ways. He introduced to Western architecture the use of panels of windows and floor heating, which he had learned about during a trip to Japan. His designs brought sunlight and the beauty of nature indoors. He got rid of boxy rooms and opened up the space inside homes. Most important, he designed buildings that fit in with their environment. Wright's goal was to be the greatest architect that ever lived. Many think he was.

Checking Comprehension

What were some of Wright's main ideas about
    architecture?

What attitude did Wright have about his work?

---

[14]extending without interruption

SIDELIGHTS

About Frank Lloyd Wright

- He changed his middle name from Lincoln to Lloyd. He also changed his birth year from 1867 to 1869!
- He once designed a mile-high skyscraper. It had 528 floors and space for 100,000 people and 15,000 cars. It was never built.
- Some of his greatest works were designed when he was in his 80s.
- One of his sons, a toy designer, created Lincoln Logs, a popular toy of the 1950s.

About Wisconsin, the Badger State

- The nickname the Badger State comes from Wisconsin's lead miners who dug into the side of a hill and lived underground, much as animal badgers do.
- The name Wisconsin comes from a Chippewa Indian word that means "gathering of waters."
- Wisconsin is known as America's Dairyland. Half of its 81,000 farms are dairy farms. They produce 40 percent of America's cheese.
- Wisconsin is a major recreation area in the Midwest. In summer, its thousands of lakes offer swimming, boating, and fishing. In winter, skiing and snowmobiling are popular sports.

Making Inferences

Reread the paragraph(s) indicated after each statement.
Then decide if each statement is probably true or false.

_____ 1. An architect does the same work as a
draftsman. (paragraphs 3, 6)

_____ 2. After the murders at Taliesin, Wright didn't want
to live in Spring Green anymore. (paragraph 16)

_____ 3. The Frank Lloyd Wright School of Architecture
has two sites so that students can work outdoors
year-round. (paragraph 23)

_____ 4. In his architectural designs, Wright liked to do
what had never been done before. (paragraphs
26, 29, Sidelights)

_____ 5. Wright's work became less innovative as he got
older. (paragraph 27, Sidelights)

Practicing Vocabulary

Circle the correct word to complete each sentence.

1. Frank Lloyd Wright was a world-famous (engineer,
architecture, architect, draftsman).
2. In the Chicago area, Wright built homes that fit the
flat midwestern landscape. So, his style of architecture
came to be called the (outdoors, natural, vertical,
prairie) style.
3. A picturesque place is very (sophisticated, scenic,
unique, hilly).
4. The murders at Taliesin were a (spiral, tragedy, risk,
symbol).
5. The people who hire an architect are called the
architect's (employees, clients, projects, contracts).

Talking It Over

1. Many people leave a place forever after they have suffered a tragedy there. Why do you think Wright stayed at Taliesin?

2. Wright once complained that he couldn't design a decent chair. Some people who have sat in Wright's chairs agree with him. Are you ever bothered by uncomfortable furniture? What advice would you give an architect who is designing furniture for a school, office, or home?

3. How important is the place where you live and the furniture you live with? Does the place where you live affect your feelings about yourself and the world?

4. What does your home say about the kind of person you are? Does it reflect your tastes, interests, and attitudes?

5. Wright defined architecture as "the truest record of life. . . ." What do you think he meant?

Thomas Alva Edison listening to his phonograph

WIZARD AT WORK

What were the first words recorded on Edison's "speaking machine," or phonograph? To find out, read on. . . .

Bright Ideas

1   In comic strips, a lightbulb over a character's head illustrates a good idea. It's a very suitable symbol. Thomas Alva Edison was the inventor of the first electric lightbulb. He had a head full of good ideas. He was, in fact, one of the greatest inventors of all time. By the time he died, at age 84, Edison had obtained patents[1] on 1,093 inventions. That's a world record.

2   The quantity of Edison's new ideas was truly amazing. But so was the quality. Henry Ford once said that 1847–1931, the span of his friend Edison's life, should be called the Age of Edison. Edison added more to the progress of technology than any other person. His discoveries led America out of the age of steam and into the age of electricity. His ideas also led to the development of the phonograph, the typewriter, the telephone, motion pictures, and

---

[1]exclusive legal rights to produce, use, and sell products using an invention for a certain number of years

the electric-powered train. And, because of the phonograph, Edison was perhaps the most famous American in the world around 1870. He was only in his mid-30s.

3   Edison was not only an inventor. He was also a businessman. He wanted to invent things that were practical and marketable. He started one of the first research laboratories in which teams of inventors worked together. He also connected the research laboratory to the manufacture of products. His West Orange, New Jersey, labs were models for the Bell and Westinghouse labs of today. The Edison Electric Company, founded in 1878, changed names several times. It became General Electric in 1892. Today it is one of the largest U.S. manufacturers.

4   Edison accomplished a lot in spite of a severe hearing loss. His hearing problems began at about age 12 and became worse as he grew older. But Edison didn't complain. In fact, he said that deafness made it easier for him to concentrate on his work.

5   Today, the best place to explore Edison's world is in his research laboratories in West Orange, New Jersey. He worked there from 1887 until his death in 1931. A tour of this national historic site teaches visitors about the beginnings of the phonograph, electric lightbulbs, and movies. It also informs visitors about the life and work habits of an extraordinary man.

Checking Comprehension

Which inventions resulted from Edison's ideas?
What did Edison accomplish besides inventing things?
What world record does Edison hold?

A Curious Boy

6   Edison was born in Milan, Ohio, in 1847. His curiosity often made life difficult for the people around him. For example, when he was six years old, he started a small fire in his father's barn. He did it to find out what would happen. He found out when the barn burned down. There are many stories about the mischief that this inquisitive[2] boy got into. Some of these stories may have been exaggerated or even invented.

7   When Edison was seven years old, his family moved to Port Huron, Michigan. He started school at that time. His teacher found him annoying because he asked so many questions. So Edison's mother decided to teach her youngest child at home.

8   Edison's mother bought him his first chemistry book. He refused to accept any of its conclusions until he did every experiment himself. His interest in chemistry grew. Soon, he had more than 100 bottles of chemicals at home.

9   At the age of 12, Edison got a job selling magazines and candy on a train. In the baggage car, he had a small chemistry lab. He also had a printing press, on which he printed a newspaper that he sold. One day, while doing an experiment with phosphorus,[3] Edison accidentally set the baggage car on fire! The conductor threw Edison, his lab, and his printing press off the train.

Checking Comprehension

What was Edison's mother's attitude toward her son's
    great curiosity?

Why did Edison get thrown off the train?

---

[2]asking many questions
[3]an element that begins to burn at very low temperatures

Early Inventions

10   After the baggage car fire, Edison worked in a train station. One day, he saved the life of a boy who ran in front of a moving freight car. The grateful father taught Edison how to operate a telegraph machine.[4] For the next six years, Edison worked as a telegrapher in the United States and Canada. During this time, Edison made many improvements on the equipment he used.

11   In 1866, Edison went to Louisville, Ohio, and was hired by Western Union. While working as a telegrapher, he thought about inventions in other fields as well. He spent 18 months in Louisville. While he was there, he made this prediction: "Someday I will give you a light that doesn't have to be lit with a match!" His stay in Louisville ended when he spilled acid on his boss's desk and got fired. But 17 years later, in 1883, he returned to Louisville to supervise the installation of some electric generators. They lit 4,600 lamps for the Southern Exposition. This important fair was the first to use Edison's electric lights.

12   Edison's first patented invention was a machine that could electrically record lawmakers' votes. He tried to sell it to the legislators[5] in Washington, D.C., but they weren't interested. Edison was disappointed. He always wanted to see his inventions being used, and he wanted to profit from them. "I always invented to obtain money to go on inventing," he said.

13   In 1869, Edison got his first big break. He was working in a New York City office that had a stock ticker.[6] He repaired and improved this machine. In fact, he owned patents on some of his design changes. One day, the president

---

[4]a device that transmits messages using a code consisting of short and long sounds
[5]people who make laws as members of a legislative body
[6]a machine that prints out changing stock prices

of the company asked Edison how much money he wanted for these patents. Edison couldn't decide if he should ask for $3,000 or $5,000. So he replied, "Suppose you make me an offer." The offer was $40,000, and he accepted it. This explains how Edison, at age 23, got enough money to go into business for himself. With this newfound wealth, Edison opened a workshop in Newark, New Jersey. There, he manufactured stock tickers and worked on improving the telegraph and the typewriter.

Checking Comprehension

Why did Edison lose his job in Louisville?
Where did he get the money to start his own business?
What were some of his early inventions?

Sound and Light

14 In 1876, Edison opened a laboratory in Menlo Park, New Jersey. He hired mechanics and chemists to work with him. He created the world's first private research and development laboratory. This lab obtained more than 400 patents.

15 Of all his inventions, his favorite and most original was the phonograph. One day, Edison was working on a device for recording telegraph messages. He noticed that sound waves could move a needle. Edison's first "talking machine" had a horn, a needle, and a copper cylinder covered with tinfoil. When someone talked into the horn, the needle vibrated and cut patterns into the tinfoil. Then, when the needle ran over those same marks, the sound was reproduced. Edison tested his new gadget by reciting the words

"Mary had a little lamb" into the horn. To Edison's great surprise, the machine played back his words. "I was always afraid of things that worked the first time," Edison said. But the phonograph made him famous and earned him his nickname, the Wizard of Menlo Park.

Edison working on a phonograph record

16   During his Menlo Park years, Edison created the first electric lightbulb. Scientists had been working on this idea for about 50 years. But the filaments[7] they used never burned long enough to make the bulb practical. Edison designed a bulb with an improved vacuum and a carbonized[8] filament made from cotton thread. On October 19, 1879, his bulb burned for 13½ hours. That date marked the beginning of the age of electric lightbulbs. But this first Edison bulb didn't last long enough for general use. So Edison sent his assistants all over the world searching for a better filament. Years later, he invented one that worked well.

17   How would people get electrical power? How would suppliers know how much electricity their customers used? To solve these problems, Edison designed the country's first electric generating station. The Pearl Street Station in New York City was completed in 1882. For it, Edison developed many new devices needed to produce and send out electrical power.

18   In 1886 and 1887, Edison moved his work to West Orange, New Jersey. There were several reasons for the change. In 1884, Edison's first wife had died, leaving him with three small children. In 1886, Edison remarried. His second wife, Mina Miller, was the daughter of a wealthy inventor and manufacturer. Edison's work required him to be in New York City often. He bought a 23-room mansion in West Orange, New Jersey, near the railroad line to New York. Edison and his second wife had three children. Today, their beautiful mansion is open to the public. Thomas and Mina Edison are buried on the grounds. The West Orange labs are just a half-mile away.

---

[7]thin material inside a lightbulb that glows when electric current goes through it
[8]treated, covered, or combined with carbon

Edison's Menlo Park, New Jersey, lab is now in Dearborn, Michigan. In 1929, Henry Ford opened a huge museum to honor American industry and technology. He moved Edison's famous lab to Greenfield Village, in Dearborn. But Ford also wanted Edison's lab to remain on New Jersey soil. So, along with the lab, he moved three carloads of New Jersey dirt! Although Edison's lab is no longer there, the town of Menlo Park hasn't forgotten its wizard. The 131-foot Edison Memorial Tower stands on the exact spot where the first practical lightbulb was made. On top of the tower is a lightbulb 14 feet high and 9 feet wide!

Edison with his lightbulbs in his laboratory

Checking Comprehension

Why was the phonograph a more original invention than the lightbulb?

What happened to Edison's Menlo Park lab?

The Invention Factory

20   Edison's West Orange facility gave him enough room to build the huge "invention factory" he'd wanted. The labs there had, Edison joked, "everything from an elephant's hide to the eyeballs of a United States senator." During the next 44 years, Edison and his staff obtained more than 600 patents on their work. Inventions were developed in the labs and then manufactured in the factories that surrounded them. In 1912, Edison had about 200 workers in his West Orange labs. By 1920, about 10,000 employees worked in his labs and factories.

21   During the West Orange years, Edison's labs developed equipment for motion pictures. The labs produced one-minute movies that people viewed (one at a time) in a machine called a kinetoscope. In 1894, the first kinetoscope parlor opened. Then people were paying to view films.

22   In 1896, Edison combined his movie camera with Thomas Armat's movie projector. As a result, movie theaters opened. In 1894, Edison had been experimenting with sound for motion pictures. By 1913, he had developed a method to give movies a voice, but it didn't catch on. Later inventors improved upon his work, and, in 1927, "talking" movies began.

23   Edison also experimented with the automobile. He believed that the car of the future would run on electricity. For about 10 years, he worked to develop an electric storage battery for cars. The batteries available at the time were very heavy, leaked power, and were difficult to recharge. By the time Edison developed a better battery, no one wanted electric cars. But Edison's battery found many mining, railroad, marine, and military uses.

24   Today's visitors to Edison's West Orange labs can almost feel the presence of the great man. In the chemistry

lab, Edison's stained, frayed lab coat is still hanging on a hook. (One Japanese tourist stood before it and bowed.) His desk is still there, too. It's covered with objects from the last few years of his life. Inventions from the Menlo Park days are also on display. These include early phonographs and lightbulbs. Visitors see *The Great Train Robbery*, one of the silent motion pictures produced in the Edison labs, made in 1903. There's also a copy of the world's first movie studio. The tour and short film give tourists insights into the personality of a man who had endless ideas.

25   What kind of person could dream up more than 1,000 inventions? Some say Edison was a genius. But it's important to remember how Edison defined the word *genius*. Genius, he said, is "1 percent inspiration and 99 percent perspiration." Edison sometimes stayed at his lab for days at a time. He would work around the clock, stopping only for short naps. His wife finally had a bed put in his office.

26   Edison's approach to solving problems was often one of trial and error. One time, a friend tried to comfort him after his 10,000 efforts to make a better battery brought no successful result. "I have not failed," Edison said. "I've just found 10,000 ways that won't work." To Edison, the question was never *if* something could be done, only *how*. And because he usually found out how things could be done, life became easier, more comfortable, and more fun for all of us.

Checking Comprehension

What were some of Edison's important accomplishments at the West Orange labs?

Why was Edison such a successful inventor?

What does Edison's definition of *genius* mean?

SIDELIGHTS

About Thomas Alva Edison

- He left over 400,000 artifacts and 5 million pages of laboratory notes, sketches, memos, and letters to friends and family.
- If his papers were stacked, they would make a pile taller than Chicago's Sears Tower.
- Scholars hope to catalog all of his works by the year 2006.
- His patents include 389 for electric light and power, 195 for the phonograph, 150 for the telegraph, 141 for storage batteries, and 34 for the telephone.

About New Jersey, the Garden State

- New Jersey is called the Garden State because of its many farms and rural scenic areas. The farms are among the nation's smallest and yet most productive.
- It is the nation's fifth smallest state in area, yet is the ninth largest in population.
- It is the most densely populated of all 50 states.
- Along the state's 127 miles of beaches is Atlantic City, which is famous for its boardwalk, the Miss America Pageant, and gambling casinos.
- Many who work in New York City make their home in New Jersey's northern suburbs.

Making Inferences

Reread the paragraph(s) indicated after each statement.
Then decide if each statement is probably true or false.

_____ 1. Edison became famous because he invented electricity. (paragraphs 2, 16–17)

_____ 2. Because he was deaf, Edison couldn't hear his phonograph play back the words "Mary Had a Little Lamb." (paragraphs 4, 15)

_____ 3. If no one wanted to use one of his inventions, Edison felt let down. (paragraph 12)

_____ 4. An inventor gets a patent so that other people cannot produce his or her invention without permission. (paragraph 1)

_____ 5. People called Edison a wizard because they thought he had magical powers. (paragraph 15)

Practicing Vocabulary

Circle the best word to complete each sentence.

1. Edison obtained patents on more than 1,000 inventions. That's a great (experiment, conductor, quantity, quality).
2. Edison was extraordinary because he was (a telegrapher, a scientist, an inventor, a genius).
3. People who are elected to make laws are called (legislators, generators, conductors, telegraphers).
4. A phonograph (reproduces, manufactures, invents, distributes) sound.
5. Edison's electric lightbulb was a great advancement because it was (frayed, accidental, rechargeable, practical).

6. A lightbulb provides (natural, extraordinary, practical, artificial) light.
7. Edison's West Orange labs formed a large research (workshop, facility, studio, mansion).

Talking It Over

1. When asked by a new employee about his lab's rules, Edison replied, "There ain't no rules around here. We're trying to accomplish something." Do you agree with Edison? Is it easier or more difficult to do good creative work when there are no rules?
2. Recently, Edison's great-granddaughter said that she admired her ancestor because he "didn't let the educational system get in the way of his curiosity." Do you think that teachers and/or parents often discourage inquisitive and creative children?
3. Would you like to work for a boss like Edison? Why or why not?
4. What would you like to invent? What do you think the world needs that hasn't been invented yet?
5. What 19th- or 20th-century invention do you think improved human life the most?

Orville Wright and Wilbur Wright working on their airplane

THE WRIGHT FLIGHT

How long did Orville Wright's first airplane flight last?
To find out, read on. . . .

A Dream of Flying

1   Kitty Hawk, North Carolina, was windy, chilly, and almost deserted. It wasn't an ideal vacation spot. But, for the Wright brothers, it was perfect. Here, they could pursue their favorite hobby, trying to realize their dream of controlled flying.

2   In 1900, Wilbur Wright sent a letter to Octave Chanute, an early believer in powered flight. For some years, Wilbur wrote, he had been "afflicted"[1] with the belief that human beings could fly. "I feel that it will soon cost me an increased amount of money, if not my life," Wilbur continued. He and Orville Wright wanted to work full-time on aviation.[2] At that time, they could do it only from September to January, when their bicycle business was slow. Wilbur Wright was looking for a good spot to test gliders.[3]

---

[1] greatly troubled by mental or physical pain
[2] the building and operation of aircraft
[3] aircraft without engines kept aloft by air currents

Chanute suggested California, Florida, South Carolina, or Georgia. All four places had sand and steady winds.

3   Wilbur Wright knew that a sandy site near an ocean was a good idea. But he also wanted a place close to his Dayton, Ohio, home. So he wrote to the National Weather Bureau for advice. The bureau told him that Kitty Hawk, North Carolina, near the Atlantic Ocean, offered ideal conditions for gliding. When Wilbur Wright found out that Kitty Hawk had a 90-foot sand dune, his choice was made.

4   Many others had risked their lives in search of the secrets of flight. How could these young men expect to find answers that had escaped older and more educated researchers? When they were boys growing up in Ohio, both boys showed great mechanical ability and a love of anything that could fly. Orville made and sold kites. The boys played with flying toys powered by twisted rubber bands.

5   After high school, neither brother went to college. First, they ran a print shop, using presses they had built themselves. Then, they opened a bicycle shop. They designed, manufactured, repaired, and sold bicycles. In their spare time, they studied about flight. Wilbur Wright was a serious, brilliant, self-taught mechanic. Orville Wright, four years younger, had more energy and stamina[4] than Wilbur. He enjoyed fashionable clothes and a good joke. Opposites in many ways, together, the brothers had the skills and determination to change the world.

Checking Comprehension

What made Kitty Hawk a good site for the Wright brothers?

What interests and skills did each of the brothers have?

---

[4]staying power and endurance

Balloons and Gliders

6   Human flight was a dream that had absorbed many people before the Wright brothers. In 1784, two French brothers developed a smoke-filled balloon that carried seven passengers in an attached basket. It climbed to about 3,000 feet and stayed up for 30 minutes. About the same time, another Frenchman developed a successful hydrogen balloon. These balloons flew because the gases inside them were lighter than air.

7   In 1891, a German aviator named Otto Lilienthal [Lil'yuhn·tawl] built and flew a glider. It looked like huge wings attached to his body. Lilienthal balanced the glider by shifting his body weight. That gave him very limited control. In 1896, his glider crashed, and he was killed. A few years later, a British pilot was killed flying a glider he had designed. Meanwhile, in the late 1890s, two Americans designed and flew a biplane[5] glider that looked like a box kite. It had some new mechanisms for control.

8   The Wright brothers studied the work of these pioneers in aviation. They also read everything available about aerodynamics [air·o·die·nam'iks].[6] In addition, they studied the world's greatest experts on flying—birds. After watching buzzards in flight, Wilbur gave his glider wing tips that could be bent up or down. When the glider began to tilt, the trailing edge of the lower wing could be twisted down and the other wing tip could be raised. They tested this theory in Dayton in 1899. It worked! It gave them control of lateral balance.[7]

9   Wilbur and Orville Wright were cautious men. They planned to test their gliders with controls operated from

---

[5]an airplane with two sets of wings one above the other
[6]the science of air and its effect on moving bodies
[7]the angle of the wings to the ground

the ground. They would fly them as kites before becoming pilots. They knew that, in order to fly safely, a pilot had to control takeoff and landing, balance, banking,[8] and turning. To do this, they had to learn about the wind's effect on flying objects.

The Wright brothers testing a glider

10   In North Carolina, the brothers hoped to find out how wind and air pressure affected flight. They considered gliding a fascinating hobby. They didn't expect to make money from it. In fact, they worried about the expense. But they didn't want investors telling them how and when to proceed. So they kept costs to a minimum and paid for their research themselves. From 1899 to 1903, the total cost of their hobby (including transportation, food, and materials) was less than $1,200! Meanwhile, one of their rivals[9] received a $100,000 government grant.

Checking Comprehension

Why was gliding dangerous?
For safety, what does a pilot need to control?
Who paid for the Wright brothers' research about gliders?

---

[8]lowering the left wing when turning left and the right wing when turning right
[9]those who compete against someone

Trying and Trying Again

11   In the fall of 1900, first 33-year-old Wilbur Wright and then 29-year-old Orville Wright went to North Carolina. The trip from Dayton to Kitty Hawk took more than a week. Kitty Hawk is on the Outer Banks of North Carolina. This narrow strip of land is almost completely surrounded by water, with the Atlantic Ocean to the east and two sounds[10] to the west.

12   The Wright brothers' exact site, Kill Devil Hills, was then part of the town of Kitty Hawk. Today, Kill Devil Hills is a separate community. How did the area get that strange name? According to local legends, either the area's rough waters or its awful rum could kill the devil.

13   During their first autumn at Kill Devil Hills, the Wright brothers lived in a tent. Later, they built two wooden hangars. One was for their glider. The other was their one-room home. They slept in hammocks[11] hung from the rafters. Their months in North Carolina were difficult, lonely, and often disappointing. They experimented, made changes in their glider's design, and tested some more. Sometimes, their changes didn't work well. Still, they kept designing, gliding, and redesigning.

14   In 1901, the brothers built the largest glider anyone had ever tried to fly. The design was based upon accepted principles of aerodynamics. Their new glider disappointed them. It didn't have the lifting power they had expected. At that point, they realized that the mathematical tables they had used were wrong. They went home to Ohio and built a small wind tunnel. (A fan provided the wind.) With it, they tested different wing shapes and angles. Then they rewrote the tables and redesigned the wings.

---

[10]narrow passages of water between islands and the mainland
[11]swinging beds made out of canvas or netting

15   Back at Kill Devil Hills, in the fall of 1902, they tried their new glider. It had better lifting power. But there was another problem. Sometimes, during a turn, the glider slid sideways and spun to the ground. Orville suggested a movable tail. Wilbur agreed. Then Wilbur suggested linking the wing and tail mechanisms to one control. They tested these changes with 1,000 more glides. Their improvements worked perfectly.

16   Now they were ready to build a plane with power. Automobile engines were too heavy for their purpose. So the Wrights designed and built a 180-pound, 12-horsepower engine. Then they made the first effective airplane propeller. The engine drove two propellers. These gave the plane enough speed to lift off. By the fall of 1903, the power-driven plane was completed. It weighed about 600 pounds. Its wooden wings were 40 feet, 4 inches long. The cloth wing coverings were made from bedsheets and sewn on their mother's sewing machine. The Wright brothers had built their amazing invention. There was only one task left—to make it fly.

Checking Comprehension

How do an airplane and a glider differ?

What work habits helped the Wright brothers succeed?

A 12-Second Flight

17   At Kill Devil Hills on December 14, 1903, the brothers were ready to test their plane the *Flyer*. They tossed a coin to select the first pilot. Wilbur Wright won. He lay down on his stomach in the middle of the plane. From that position, he could operate some of the controls by moving his body from side to side. He started the engine. The *Flyer* left the

ground. Because of steering mistakes, it climbed too steeply, stopped, and fell onto the sand. It took two days to repair the damage.

18   On December 17, it was Orville Wright's turn to fly. Only five people came to watch. One of them was asked to stand near the box camera and take a photo when the plane lifted off the ground. The airplane took off at 10:35 A.M. and flew for 12 seconds. The man with the camera became very excited. After the flight, he couldn't remember if he had taken the photograph or not. Back in Dayton, a few days later, Orville developed and printed the picture. It showed the *Flyer* just after liftoff, flying into a 24-mile-per-hour wind.

The Wright brothers' airplane, the Flyer

19   After Orville's flight, the brothers took turns flying the plane. They had four successful flights that day. The fourth flight lasted 59 seconds and covered 852 feet. Later, they described their achievement as "very modest compared with that of the birds." But, for human beings, it was a historic accomplishment.

20   Later that day, the brothers sent a telegram to their father. It said, "SUCCESS STOP FOUR FLIGHTS THURSDAY MORNING STOP HOME CHRISTMAS." That same day, a strong wind blew the *Flyer* over. It was badly damaged and never flew again. In December of 1948, it was hung in the National Air and Space Museum in Washington, D.C. It is still there—hanging higher above the ground than it ever flew.

Checking Comprehension

What was the date of the historic first flight?
What did the Wright brothers accomplish?
Where is the *Flyer* now?

Troubles and Tributes

21   The Wright brothers' successful flights did not bring instant fame and fortune. It took about five years before the general public realized their importance. For the next two years, the Wright brothers continued their experimental flights. In 1905, the *Flyer III* flew 25 miles in 38 minutes.

22   That year, the Wright brothers tried to interest the United States government in their invention. But they were turned down. For the next few years, they didn't fly at all, fearing that their invention might be stolen. Finally, in 1908, the Wrights signed contracts with the American and the French governments to build the first military aircraft.

23   That same year, Wilbur Wright was in France making flights at altitudes of 300 feet. Meanwhile, Orville Wright was setting flight records in the United States. On September 9, he made 57 complete circles over a Virginia airfield. Eight days later, a loose wire wrapped around a propeller blade, and Orville's plane crashed. Orville broke several bones, and his passenger was killed. Orville recovered completely. A year later, he and his brother were giving flying lessons and organizing two companies to make planes. But legal problems such as patent infringements[12] and lawsuits continued to trouble them.

24   Wilbur Wright died of typhoid fever in 1912. Orville Wright continued to do research in aviation until his death in 1948. He lived to see "the miracle at Kitty Hawk" become a major form of transportation. He also attended the 1932 dedication of the Wright Brothers National Memorial.

25   The Wright brothers had lived most of their lives in Dayton, Ohio. Today, the city has many sites to show tourists. The brothers' bicycle shop is now a museum. The *Flyer III* is on exhibit at a local historic park.

26   Kill Devil Hills, North Carolina, is the home of the Wright Brothers National Memorial. Inside the visitor's center is a model of the *Flyer* with Orville Wright at the controls. A park ranger shows visitors how the brothers controlled the plane. After seeing the exhibits, some visitors get hooked on flight. They sign up for an aerial sightseeing tour or a hang gliding lesson.

---

[12]unlawful use of inventions that have been protected by legal rights

27   Outside, a stone marks the spot where the *Flyer* took off. Four more stones mark the four December 17th landings. Nearby are reproductions of the wooden hangars where the brothers lived and kept their gliders. On Big Kill Devil Hill, the sand dune from which their gliders took off, a six-story pylon[13] honors their achievement. Overhead, jet planes zoom across the sky, using the principles of flight that the Wright brothers tested and proved.

Checking Comprehension

What problems did the brothers have after their successful 1903 flights?
Was "the miracle at Kitty Hawk" really a miracle?
What can tourists see in Kill Devil Hills?

---

[13]a tall towerlike structure

SIDELIGHTS

About Orville and Wilbur Wright

- Neither brother ever married.
- The brothers dressed in suits and ties even when launching gliders from a sand dune.
- The Wrights didn't use the word *airplane*. They called their invention a "flyer."
- The Wright brothers built the *Flyer* for less than $1,000. The U.S. government spent $500,000 building a model.
- How high did the *Flyer* fly? Not more than 15 feet above the ground.

About North Carolina, the Tarheel State

- The nickname the Tarheel State dates back to colonial days when North Carolina was a leading producer of tar and turpentine.
- In honor of the Wright brothers, North Carolina's license plates read "First in Flight."
- Cape Hatteras in the Outer Banks is called the "graveyard of the Atlantic" because so many shipwrecks have occurred there.
- The first English settlement in America was established in 1585 on Roanoke Island, North Carolina.
- The nation's largest private residence, the 250-room Biltmore Estate, is in Asheville, North Carolina. It was built for George Washington Vanderbilt in 1895.

Making Inferences

Reread the paragraph(s) indicated after each statement.
Then decide if each statement is probably true or false.

_____ 1. Wilbur Wright's prediction about his death came true. (paragraphs 2, 24)

_____ 2. Gliders fly because they are lighter than air. (paragraphs 6–7)

_____ 3. The Wright brothers built the first glider. (paragraph 7)

_____ 4. The Wright brothers paid for their experiments because no one else offered them any money. (paragraph 10)

_____ 5. The *Flyer* was a glider. (paragraph 16)

_____ 6. Cameras were invented before airplanes. (paragraph 18)

_____ 7. On December 17, 1903, Wilbur Wright flew the fourth flight of the day. (paragraphs 18, 19)

Practicing Vocabulary

Circle the correct answer to each question.

1. Which of the following words does not describe the Wright brothers?

   inventors   pilots   pioneers   propellers

2. Which is not part of an airplane?

   engine   hangar   tail   wing

3. What does an airplane have that a glider does not?

   a pilot   an engine   a tail   controls

4. Where did the Wright brothers sleep during their first autumn in Kill Devil Hills?

in a glider   in hammocks   in a tent   on the beach

5. Which of the following flies because gases make it lighter than air?

a butterfly   a kite   a glider   a balloon

Talking It Over

1. What is your favorite hobby? Why do you enjoy it?
2. "If at first you don't succeed, try, try again" is a well-known saying. Do you think Orville and Wilbur Wright followed it? Is it always good advice?
3. In what ways has the airplane helped human beings? How has it harmed them?
4. What other famous pairs of people accomplished something important? See how many you can list in three minutes.
5. Air travel is the safest form of travel. Why do you think this is so?

Writer and philosopher Henry David Thoreau at age 37

A DIFFERENT DRUMMER

Why did Henry David Thoreau have a library of 700 books—all written by himself? To find out, read on....

The Simple Life

1   It was just a pond. Could it teach a person how to live? One unusual young man decided to find out. The man was Henry David Thoreau [Thor·oh']. The place was Walden Pond in Concord, Massachusetts. The year was 1845. At the age of 27, Thoreau decided to build a small cabin near the pond and live there alone. That's how Walden Pond became the site of a famous experiment. The result was the creation of a masterpiece, one of the great works of American literature.

2   Why did Thoreau come to Walden? He wanted to study nature and write about it. But he was also testing his views about life. Thoreau didn't think that other people lived properly. He watched them work hard in order to have a lot of possessions they didn't need. He noticed that people were too busy to enjoy the beauty of nature.

3   Thoreau decided to try another approach to life. He wanted to simplify his needs and get along with as little as

possible. That would make him rich in the two ways he valued greatly. He would have freedom and time to pursue his own interests.

Checking Comprehension

According to Thoreau, what was wrong with the way most people lived?

What things made for a happy life in Thoreau's opinion?

Before Walden Pond

4   What kind of person would choose to live alone in the woods? Thoreau was a scientist, civil engineer, and writer. A Harvard graduate, he could speak several languages. This brilliant scholar came from a very ordinary and poor family. His father had a small pencil-making business. His mother took in boarders to add to the family income. But his parents instilled in their children a love of nature and learning, as well as a strong moral sense.

5   Thoreau developed his manual skills. He became a carpenter, gardener, and handyman. At various times in his life, he supported himself with these skills. At other times, he worked as a surveyor[1] or as a pencil maker.

6   Thoreau and his brother John Thoreau were close. They enjoyed the outdoors together. Thoreau's first published book, *A Week on the Concord and Merrimack Rivers*, was about their boating adventures in 1838. On that trip, Thoreau decided to be a poet of nature.

7   In 1837, after Thoreau graduated from Harvard, he got a job teaching in a local school. A member of the school

---

[1]a person who measures land

committee tried to interfere with the way Thoreau was teaching. After two weeks on the job, he quit. He and his brother opened their own school. At their school, learning was to be a positive experience. Students were not punished with a stick. The brothers believed that young people would learn more if they enjoyed their studies.

8   In 1840, Thoreau proposed marriage to an attractive Concord visitor, Ellen Sewall. But, following the advice of her father, she did not marry Thoreau. In later years, Thoreau had many other women friends. But he remained a bachelor all his life.

9   The Thoreau brothers' school operated successfully for a few years. Then John Thoreau got tuberculosis.[2] The school was closed so that he could have complete rest. In 1842, he was recovering from TB when he cut his finger while shaving. The cut became infected. A few days later, John Thoreau died of lockjaw.[3] Thoreau was so disturbed by this loss that he briefly suffered from his brother's symptoms. After his brother's death, Henry Thoreau didn't want to return to teaching. He worked in the family business but didn't enjoy it.

10   Thoreau's friend, the noted author and orator[4] Ralph Waldo Emerson, helped the young man get back to writing. The two Concord authors had become friends in 1837. Emerson was 14 years older and already doing well in his career when Thoreau returned to Concord as a college graduate. Emerson encouraged Thoreau to keep a journal.

---

[2]a lung disease (also called TB)
[3]a condition in which the jaws become firmly closed because of muscle contractions
[4]a public speaker

In 1845, when Thoreau decided that he wanted to live alone and close to nature, Emerson offered him the perfect spot. It was Walden Pond. This small lake, two miles from the center of Concord, was on land that Emerson owned.

Checking Comprehension

What did Henry and John Thoreau have in common?
What was unusual about their school?
What were some of Henry Thoreau's major interests?

The Necessities of Life

11   At Walden, Thoreau wanted to live without luxuries. He wanted to lead a simple life. His first task was to figure out what things were absolutely necessary. He realized that food, clothing, shelter, and fuel were all he needed in order to survive. Once he had these, Thoreau said, he could think about the true problems of life with a sense of freedom.

12   In March 1845, Thoreau borrowed an ax from a friend and cut down some white pine trees near Walden Pond. He built a small house only 10 feet wide and 15 feet long with an attic and a cellar. The house had one door, which was never locked. It had two windows, with no curtains. He was willing, he said, to let the sun and moon look in on him.

13   The cabin had a few pieces of furniture. Some were handmade, some borrowed from friends and family. Thoreau brought a few cooking utensils and tools, including a knife, an ax, a spade, and a wheelbarrow. He also brought a few books, paper and pen, and an oil lamp.

14   The cabin provided shelter. Clothing was not important to Thoreau. In fact, he wrote, "Sell your clothes and keep your thoughts." He didn't care about looking stylish. He dressed in durable, comfortable clothing.

The simplicity of Thoreau's cabin

15   Food and fuel were readily available. Walden Pond provided clean water to drink. When he needed wood for fuel, he dug up old tree stumps. Food was no problem, either. He bought some basic supplies from the store—such as flour, rice, and salt. He caught fish in the pond. Berries grew nearby. Thoreau also had a vegetable garden and a field of beans. Once, he killed a woodchuck[5] for stealing from his garden. Later, he was sorry. The beans belonged to the woodchucks as much as to him, Thoreau realized.

16   While he was at Walden, Thoreau didn't isolate himself from others. Sometimes people came to visit. At other times he went to friends' houses for dinner. Every few days, he walked into town for supplies. But, many days, animals were his only companions. In one case, he made friends

---

[5]a small, furry animal also called a groundhog

with a mouse. A person could be lonelier in a crowd than home alone, he wrote. Thoreau liked people, but he also had a great need for privacy. He needed time alone to get his thoughts down on paper.

Checking Comprehension

What four things were necessary for Thoreau's survival?
What freedom did Thoreau gain by living at Walden?
Are being alone and being lonely the same thing?

The Seasons at Walden Pond

17   Thoreau worked hard at Walden, but he didn't consider his activities work. He fished and farmed. He watched, listened to, and took notes on his environment. In his journals, he described the four seasons of his first year there.

18   During the summer, Thoreau bathed in the pond every morning. He cleaned his house by pulling his furniture outside onto the grass. Then he scrubbed the floor with water and sand from the pond. He watched birds, frogs, and other small animals that lived around Walden Pond.

19   In autumn, he was busy gathering grapes, apples, and nuts to store for the winter. He loved to watch the leaves change colors. Then, when they fell off the trees, he enjoyed hiking through the dry leaves. When the temperature dropped below freezing, he plastered his house with sand to keep out the cold winds. He built a fireplace in his cabin and began to cook indoors. In late autumn, after the pond froze, he crawled out onto the ice and looked down. He could see all the way to the bottom. It was "like a picture behind glass," he wrote.

20   Winter brought cold and snow. Thoreau enjoyed a "merry snowstorm." When snowflakes blew wildly outside, he felt cheerful beside his fireplace. In winter, his main

outdoor activity was collecting firewood. That sometimes required long hikes through the deep snow. One winter, some moles moved into his cellar and ate "every third potato." But Thoreau didn't bother them.

21   One day, Thoreau wrote in his journal, "The sun shines bright and warm this first spring morning, re-creating the world." Spring brought melting snow, fog, rain, and the return of the birds. Thoreau was especially glad to have "the leisure and the opportunity to watch the spring come in." Most people, he knew, didn't take time to really notice and enjoy this wonderful experience.

Checking Comprehension

Which season do you think Thoreau liked best?
In which season was he the busiest?
How did he feel about the animals of the woods?

Important Works

22   Thoreau lived beside Walden Pond for two years, two months, and two days. Why did he leave? Perhaps because he had "several more lives to live." When he left, his journals were full of notes that later became two published books. One of these books was about his boat trip with his brother. Thoreau himself had to pay for its publication. It sold only 200 copies. His publisher eventually shipped the remaining 700 copies to Thoreau. The author then joked about his large library mostly written by himself.

23   The other book was called *Walden*. Thoreau worked on *Walden* for eight years. He wrote seven different drafts! Finally, in 1854, *Walden* was published. It sold merely 2,000 copies in its first five years. No other books by Thoreau were published during his lifetime. But he did publish about 60 newspaper and magazine articles. He died of

tuberculosis in 1862, at the age of 44. Today, *Walden* is widely read all over the world. It is admired for the power of its ideas and the beauty of its writing style. *Walden* is an adventure story, a how-to book, a study of nature, and a book about economics. In addition, it is a study of morality.[6] The narrator describes a way of life he considers to be in harmony with nature and with God.

24   Besides *Walden*, Thoreau's most important work was the essay "Civil Disobedience." Thoreau strongly opposed slavery. He also opposed the Mexican-American War, which he considered a means of expanding slavery in the United States. He refused to pay his poll tax[7] to the state of Massachusetts because it wasn't doing enough to end slavery. As a result, Thoreau was arrested and put in jail in July 1846. He spent only one night there. The next morning, someone paid the tax for him, but he wasn't happy about it. This brief time behind bars became the basis of "Civil Disobedience."

25   The essay, published in 1849, encouraged people to disobey immoral laws. This act is called passive resistance. The great Russian writer and social reformer Leo Tolstoy, Indian leader Mohandas Gandhi, and American civil rights leader Martin Luther King Jr. were influenced by Thoreau's writing. They all believed in disobeying evil laws as a way of reacting to injustice.

Checking Comprehension

What kind of a book is *Walden*?

Why wasn't Thoreau pleased when someone paid his overdue taxes?

How have Thoreau's ideas affected 20th-century history?

---

[6]what is right and wrong (or good and bad) behavior
[7]a tax of a fixed amount per person levied on adults

26   Walden Woods and Walden Pond still exist. They offer 500,000 visitors a year a pleasant retreat in the wilderness. Many come to spend time walking around the pond. Some add a stone to the pile that marks the former location of Thoreau's cabin. Joggers, hikers, picnickers, swimmers, fishermen, and writers enjoy Walden Woods.

Walden Pond in Concord, Massachusetts

27   In recent years, developers have tried to buy parts of Walden Woods. They planned to construct office or apartment buildings on the land. An organization called the Walden Woods Project has been peacefully resisting. Many important people in government, the arts, and entertainment have been raising funds to help this organization buy the land and save Walden Woods. Benefit concerts, walkathons, and T-shirt sales have raised some of the money. Some people also donate to the cause by buying maple trees grown from seeds found in Walden Woods. Thoreau once said, "In wildness is the preservation of the world."

Those who believe him are trying hard to keep Walden Woods wild.

28   An international organization—the Thoreau Society—teaches people about Thoreau's ideas. The Thoreau Lyceum [Lie·see'um][8] in Concord has classes, lectures, exhibits, publications, and nature walks all related to Thoreau. On the lyceum's grounds, there is even a copy of Thoreau's Walden Pond cabin.

29   Today, Thoreau is widely recognized as a forerunner of the American conservation[9] movement because of his writings. Thoreau realized, for example, that railroads brought not just fast transportation but also dirtier air. He urged people to live in harmony with the environment and respect all forms of life. Today, many people worry about pollution and endangered animals. They recognize Thoreau's amazing foresight.

30   In *Walden*, Thoreau wrote this famous defense of the unconventional[10] person: "If a man does not keep pace with his companions, perhaps it is because he hears a different drummer. Let him step to the music which he hears, however measured or far away." His words still speak to us today as each person tries to discover his or her own uniqueness.

Checking Comprehension

Is Thoreau's cabin still standing beside Walden Pond?
Why do people visit Walden Pond today?
What were some of Thoreau's beliefs?
Who or what is the "different drummer"?

---

[8]an organization providing public lectures and other educational and cultural activities
[9]the care and protection of natural resources
[10]not following the usual social customs

SIDELIGHTS

About Henry David Thoreau

- Thoreau grew up in an antislavery family. His parents' attic was a stop on the Underground Railroad (a hideout for runaway slaves).
- The poll tax debt that sent Thoreau to jail was about $4.50 ($1.50 a year).
- Thoreau's complete journals, published in 1906, include 14 volumes, about two million words!

About Concord

- The American Revolutionary War began in Concord with "the shot heard round the world," on April 19, 1775.
- In the 1800s, Concord was home to several important writers: Thoreau, Emerson, Nathaniel Hawthorne, and Louisa May Alcott. All are buried in Concord's Sleepy Hollow Cemetery, a popular tourist site.

About Massachusetts, the Bay State

- It was given the nickname the Bay State because of the early settlers on Cape Cod Bay.
- The name Massachusetts comes from the Algonquin Indian word that means "under the great mountain," which refers to the Blue Hills near Milton.

Making Inferences

Reread the paragraph(s) indicated after each statement.
Then decide if each statement is probably true or false.

_____ 1. Thoreau believed that the less a person had and needed, the richer that person was. (paragraphs 2–3)

_____ 2. Thoreau wanted more leisure time because he was lazy and had no ambition. (paragraphs 2–7)

_____ 3. Thoreau approved of the common 19th-century practice of hitting students when they didn't behave well or study hard in school. (paragraph 7)

_____ 4. When he lived in Walden Woods, Thoreau needed a gun to protect him from the dangerous wild animals there. (paragraphs 12, 15–16, 18)

_____ 5. Because he was highly educated, Thoreau didn't think he should do any physical labor. (paragraphs 5, 12, 15, 17–20)

_____ 6. Thoreau became famous during his lifetime. (paragraph 23)

_____ 7. Although he died more than 100 years ago, Thoreau's writings deal with modern American problems. (paragraphs 24–25, 27, 29–30)

Practicing Vocabulary

Circle the correct word or phrase to complete each sentence.

1. Ralph Waldo Emerson (owed, owned, rented, borrowed) property in Walden Woods.

2. At Walden, sometimes an animal was Thoreau's only (collection, convention, companion, combination).

3. A masterpiece is (an outstanding work, a very long work, an author's favorite work, a fine piece of writing).
4. An orator communicates by (writing, speaking, whistling, dancing).
5. A luxury is something that is (essential, fancy, not needed, comfortable).

Talking It Over

1. Which of Thoreau's ideas do you agree or disagree with most? Why?
2. Have you ever spent 24 hours totally alone, without talking to anyone, not even on the phone? Could you do it and not feel lonely?
3. Is it good or bad for people to enjoy their own company more than the company of other people?
4. Do you think that civil disobedience is an effective way to bring about social and political change? How did Mohandas Gandhi use this method in India? How did Martin Luther King Jr. use it in the United States? Did their efforts work?
5. What other ways are there to bring about change besides civil disobedience?

ANSWER KEY

EARTH MOTHER

Making Inferences, page 14

1. False. She was lonely because she was the youngest child. She was also shy.
2. False. The book didn't sell well because World War II began just after it was published.
3. True.
4. False. Scientists did not yet know the harmful effects of DDT.
5. True.
6. True.
7. False. Many studied ecology and other related fields.

Practicing Vocabulary, page 14

1. an ocean 2. related 3. the shore 4. deadly
5. the science of life 6. came true 7. man-made

Talking It Over, page 15

1. Answers will vary.
2. Answers will vary.
3. Answers will vary. You might think of recycling or other projects that help the environment or of times when you share the enjoyment of nature with your friends and family.
4. Answers will vary. You might state that young women can be anything they desire to be. However, certain professions are still difficult for women to enter.
5. Answers will vary. If you live in an urban community, empty lots might be a common problem. Possible solutions might include organizing cleanups and planting community gardens.

DR. KING'S DREAM

Making Inferences, page 30

1. False. Sometimes he disobeyed his parents, about doing dishes, for example.
2. True.
3. False. She was not a minister. But she had experienced racial injustice firsthand.
4. False. Sometimes others used violence against his nonviolent activities.

5. False. Sit-ins can occur in any public location.
6. True.
7. False. They think it is in questionable taste since it traces the path of the deadly bullet that killed King.

Practicing Vocabulary, page 30
1. minister
2. refuse
3. sacrifice
4. guaranteed
5. celebrate
6. chronological
7. despair
8. dedicated

Talking It Over, page 31
1. Answers will vary.
2. Answers will vary. You might agree that knowledge and faith are necessary for success in life. Added qualities might be diligence, hard work, and even luck.
3. Answers will vary.
4. Answers will vary. If King were alive today, he might be pleased with the increase in elected African-American officials, more middle-class African-American families, and more integration than in the 1960s. On the negative side, he might note today's high unemployment rate, continued poverty, increased crime, and greater drug use.
5. Answers will vary.
6. Answers will vary.

THE HOUSE THAT WRIGHT BUILT

Making Inferences, page 44
1. False. A draftsman executes an architect's ideas in accurate measurements.
2. False. He wanted to live there but make changes in the building.
3. True.
4. True.
5. False. The Guggenheim Museum, which was completed after Wright's death, was a very innovative design. Some of his greatest works were designed when Wright was in his 80s.

Practicing Vocabulary, page 44
1. architect
2. prairie
3. scenic
4. tragedy
5. clients

Talking It Over, page 45
1. Answers will vary. Perhaps Wright needed the security of familiar surroundings. Also, this area had been an important part of his life from early childhood.
2. Answers will vary.
3. Answers will vary.
4. Answers will vary. You might think people's homes reflect their attitudes and also influence them. Some people prefer the grandeur of large rooms and high ceilings. They may think that kind of home would encourage a formal manner. Others prefer the intimacy of smaller rooms with low ceilings. They may have found it encourages a relaxed, casual manner.
5. Answers will vary.

WIZARD AT WORK

Making Inferences, page 58
1. False. He neither invented nor discovered electricity. He made the first practical lightbulb and built the first major electric power station.
2. False. He heard it. At the time he invented the phonograph, he was hard of hearing but not totally deaf.
3. True.
4. True.
5. False. People knew that he was a scientist, not a magician. But his inventions were so amazing that people thought of him as a wizard.

Practicing Vocabulary, page 58
1. quantity
2. a genius
3. legislators
4. reproduces
5. practical
6. artificial
7. facility

Talking It Over, page 59
1. Answers will vary. You might think that rules are not always bad. They can provide a framework that steers creative efforts in the direction needed. But too many rules and limitations can get in the way of creative ideas.
2. Answers will vary.
3. Answers will vary.
4. Answers will vary.
5. Answers will vary.

THE WRIGHT FLIGHT

Making Inferences, page 72

1. False. He didn't die as a result of flying. He died of typhoid fever.
2. False. Gliders are not lighter than air, but they do float on air currents.
3. False. In 1891, Lilienthal built and flew a glider. The Wright brothers built the first powered flying machine.
4. False. They were offered money, but they refused it. They wanted to be independent and not have other people telling them how and when to conduct their experiments.
5. False. It wasn't a glider because it had an engine.
6. True. There was a camera on site to photograph the takeoff of the Wright brothers' *Flyer.*
7. True. Orville and Wilbur took turns. Orville flew the first and third flights. Wilbur flew the second and fourth flights.

Practicing Vocabulary, page 72

1. propellers
2. hangar
3. an engine
4. in a tent
5. a balloon

Talking It Over, page 73

1. Answers will vary.
2. Answers will vary. You might answer that Orville and Wilbur Wright didn't give up. They kept trying. They learned from their experiences and kept making improvements. It is an approach we can use in our lives as well.
3. Answers will vary. On the positive side, airplanes have made it easier for people to travel all over the world. On the negative side, in wartime, airplanes with bombs cause great destruction and human suffering.
4. Answers will vary. Some famous pairs include comedians Laurel and Hardy and Abbott and Costello, scientists Pierre and Marie Curie, and composers Gilbert and Sullivan and Rodgers and Hammerstein.
5. Answers will vary. Some reasons why air travel is safe include that there are high standards for airplane pilots, that technicians are well-trained, and that there is greater distance between airplanes than between cars.

A DIFFERENT DRUMMER

Making Inferences, page 86
1. True.
2. False. He wanted time free from work in order to write, study nature, and enjoy the beauty of his surroundings.
3. False. He believed that learning should be a positive experience for students.
4. False. The animals Thoreau came across in Walden Woods were small animals and not dangerous.
5. False. He did a lot of physical labor and found some of it satisfying.
6. False. His reputation as an important writer did not begin until after his death.
7. True. His concerns about whether human beings were damaging the environment is now the subject of an important field of study called ecology. His desire to preserve the wilderness and respect and protect all forms of life are important concerns today.

Practicing Vocabulary, page 86
1. owned
2. companion
3. an outstanding work
4. speaking
5. not needed

Talking It Over, page 87
1. Answers will vary.
2. Answers will vary.
3. Answers will vary.
4. Answers will vary. You might think that civil disobedience has worked many times in the past, but it also disrupts life wherever it occurs. People practicing civil disobedience are often put in jail. Gandhi used civil disobedience to force the English not to treat Indians as second-class citizens. His efforts led to Indian independence from British control. King used sit-ins and other forms of civil disobedience to oppose racial segregation. These actions helped bring about peaceful change.
5. Answers will vary. Your answer may include electing different people to office and using the courts to decide cases involving important social issues. Also, writings can alter public opinion and lead to social change.